D0579914

Welcome, Reader!

Do you like to teach your pet tricks? Do you like to solve mysteries? Would you like to look for creatures in the sea? In this book you will read about characters who do these things and more.

Get ready to read new words and meet new people.

Let's read together, and

Let's Be Friends!

Houghton Mifflin
Reading

Let's Be Friends

Senior Authors
J. David Cooper
John J. Pikulski

Authors
David J. Chard
Gilbert Garcia
Claude Goldenberg
Phyllis Hunter
Marjorie Y. Lipson
Shane Templeton
Sheila Valencia
MaryEllen Vogt

Consultants
Linda H. Butler
Linnea C. Ehri
Carla Ford

HOUGHTON MIFFLIN   BOSTON

Let's Look Around!

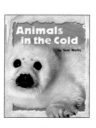

Let's Look Around!

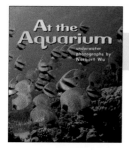

Theme 4

Family and Friends

Family and Friends

Read Together

Let's Look Around!

Sleeping Outdoors

Under the dark is a star,
Under the star is a tree,
Under the tree is a blanket,
And under the blanket is me.

by Marchette Chute

11

Stories to Read

❶ Get Set Story

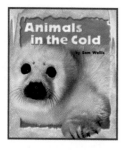

Nonfiction

❷ Main Story

Nonfiction

❸ Language Arts Link

Nonfiction

Words to Know

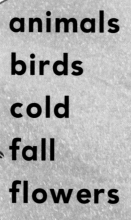

animals	full	is
birds	look	lots
cold	of	pick
fall	see	pups
flowers	buds	will

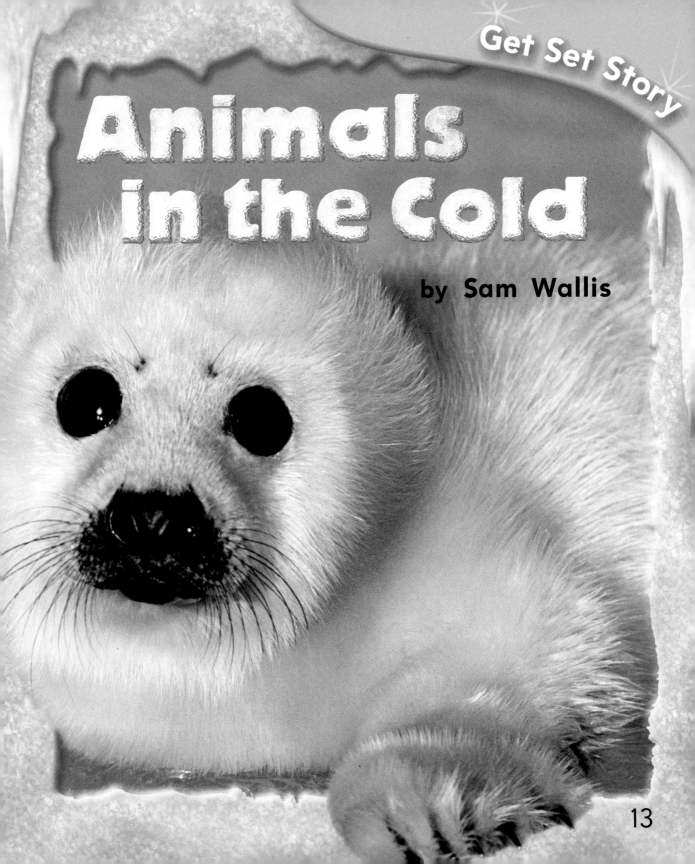

Animals in the Cold

by Sam Wallis

It is cold here. It is not hot
in the sun.

Lots of animals live here.
They do not see buds and flowers.

Look! A big animal can dig a den.
It can pick up its cub and go in.

Birds fall in and go for a dip.
They will get wet.

A den is full of fox pups.

They are not cold in the den.

Meet the Author and Illustrator

Ashley Wolff grew up in the country. She has always loved to watch and draw animals.

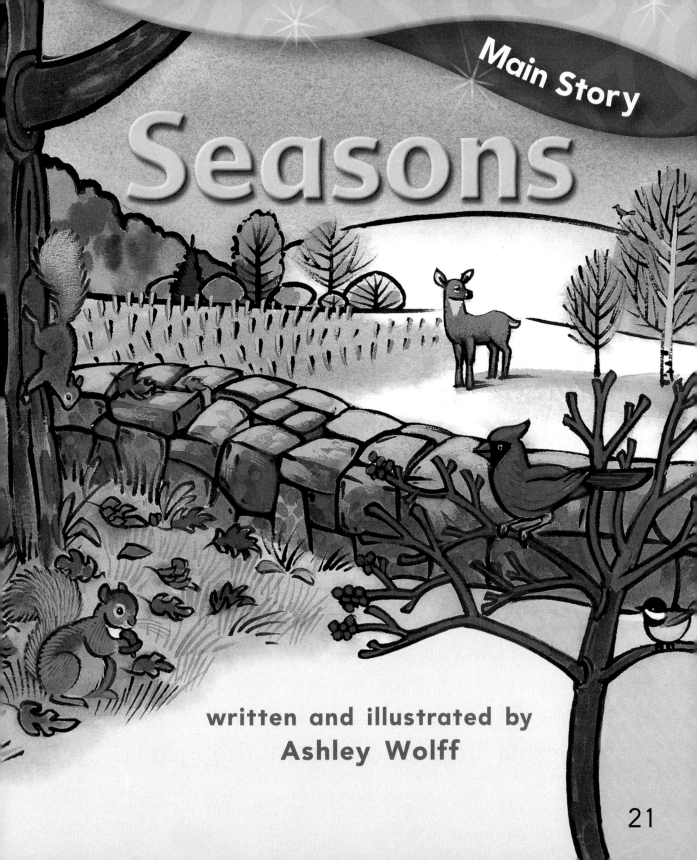

Seasons

written and illustrated by
Ashley Wolff

Spring

It is spring.
Animals hop and run in the grass.

Trees are full of buds.
Nests are full of eggs.

23

It will rain in the spring.
Look who can jump and kick
in the mud!

24

The flower buds are wet.
They will get big in the sun.

Summer

It is summer.
Look who is here!
Three birds are in the nest.

Insects see lots of flowers.
They buzz and buzz in the
hot sun.

27

It is not too hot here.
Ducks quack and quack in
a pond.

Two fox pups get a sip.
Lots of animals are here at
the end of summer.

Fall

It is fall.

Lots and lots of red leaves fall.
Animals run and play.

A buck has to get fat for a
cold winter.

Look who can pick up nuts!
They get set for the cold, too.

Winter

It is winter.

It can get cold and wet.

Where do animals go?

Birds can go south.

Lots of animals will nap in winter.
A bear will nap in a den.

Look who has a winter nap, too!
It is not cold and wet in here.

The cold winter will pass.
Animals will look for spring.

Think About the Story

Seasons

1 How did the animals get ready for the four seasons?

2 What did you learn about winter?

3 What happens during the seasons where you live?

Retell the Story

Work with three classmates. Each of you should choose a season. Tell what happens during your season.

Write a Sentence

Write a sentence about your favorite season.

I can swim in the summer.

Ha! Ha! Ha!

Why does Duck's roof leak
when it rains in the spring?

Because the roof has lots of
quacks in it!

Jack: I have corn growing out
of my ears this summer!

Jill: How did that happen?

Jack: I don't know! I planted
carrots!

43

Seasons Song

Winter, spring, summer, fall,
Which one is the best of all?

Winter has the cold and snow.
Spring has rain so flowers grow.

Summer has the hot, hot sun.
Fall has school and friends and fun.

45

Stories to Read

① Get Set Story

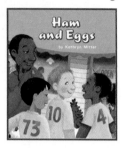

Realistic
Fiction

② Main Story

Fantasy

③ Social Studies Link

Nonfiction

Words to Know

all	first	fixed
called	never	Jack's
eat	paper	licked
eating	shall	yelled
every	why	

Ham and Eggs

by Kathryn Mitter

"Dad, can we eat at Jack's?" I said.
"Why not?" said Dad.

"I never go to Jack's," said Ted.
"It is fun here."

"Here is Jack," said Dad.
Jack had a pen and paper.
"What will you have?" Jack said.
"Let Ted go first," Dad said.

"I shall have ham and eggs,"
Ted said.
"Ham and eggs! Ham and eggs!"
we yelled.

Jack fixed us ham and eggs.
"Eat up!" called Jack.
"Yum, yum!" said Ted.

Ted licked his lips.
We had every bit of ham and eggs.
We ALL had fun eating at Jack's.

53

Meet the Author

Nancy Shaw likes to write stories that make children laugh. Many of her stories are about animals doing silly things.

Meet the Illustrator

Margot Apple has four cats and three horses. She loves spending time with her horses and drawing pictures.

Miss Jill's Ice Cream Shop

written by Nancy Shaw
illustrated by Margot Apple

Bill and Jack went to Miss
Jill's shop.

"Look at all the ice cream!" said Jack.
"What shall I eat first?"

"Try eating the green ice cream,"
said Bill.

"Why not?" said Jack.

"Miss Jill, what do you call it?"

"It is mint," said Miss Jill.
She fixed Jack a mint cone.

"I will have plum in a dish," said Bill.
"He likes lots of nuts on top,"
said Jack.

60

Miss Jill filled Bill's dish and
dumped nuts on top.

"Yum!" said Jack.

"I will have plum, too."

"Here you go!" said Miss Jill.

Jack licked his lips.
"I will have every kind," he said.
Miss Jill added ice cream to
Jack's cone.

"You will never eat it all," said Bill.
"Yes, I will!" said Jack.

Jack had his first big lick.
"Look!" yelled Bill. "It is falling!"

Jack bumped Bill.
Bill fell, and up went his ice cream.
Ice cream fell on all of the animals.

Miss Jill ran to get paper napkins.
She fell, too.

"What a mess!" yelled Bill.
"I can help!"

"Run! Run!" yelled the animals.

"I wish I had asked for a dish,"
said Jack.

Think About the Story

**Miss Jill's
Ice Cream Shop**

1 What kind of ice cream did Jack get first?

2 How did ice cream get on all of the animals?

3 What do you think Jack will get at Miss Jill's next time? Why?

Retell the Story

Act out the story with
two classmates. Use masks.

Write a Menu

Write a menu for Miss
Jill's shop. Draw
pictures for the menu.

dish

cone

brownie
sundae

Read
Together

Making Ice Cream

Do you know how ice cream
is made? Here are the steps.
Milk, cream, sugar, and flavors
are all mixed in a big tank.

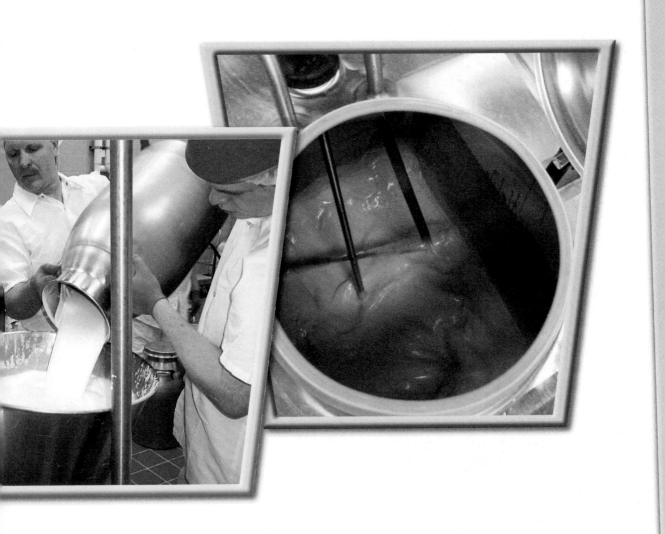

The mix is heated to get rid
of germs. Then the hot mix is
cooled. Big blades stir in air
to make the mix soft and fluffy.

Things like cookie bits and chips get added last. The ice cream is put into tubs. The tubs go into a freezer.

Trucks bring the ice cream to
stores. What flavor will you eat?

Stories to Read

❶ Get Set Story

Fantasy

❷ Main Story

Nonfiction

❸ Drama Link

Play

Words to Know

also	green	grass
blue	like	it's
brown	many	let's
colors	some	trip
funny	grab	

The Trip

by Lynne Chapman

Museum of Mouse Art

Puff and Tip went on a trip.
Dad and Mom went also.
"Grab a bus pass and hop on!"
said Dad.

"Look at the big brown cats!"
yelled Tip.
"Let's go in," said Mom.

"I see some cats!" yelled Tip.
"I see many cats," added Puff.

"Look at all the colors on the
cats!" yelled Tip.
"I like the blue and green cat,"
added Puff. "It's funny."

83

Tip and Puff sat on the grass.
"Where is the bus?" said Mom.
"Let's get a cab," said Puff.

"Here we are," said Mom.
"What a trip!" added Puff.

Meet the Photographer

Norbert Wu dives into the sea to take pictures of the amazing things that live there. He uses a special camera to take the pictures.

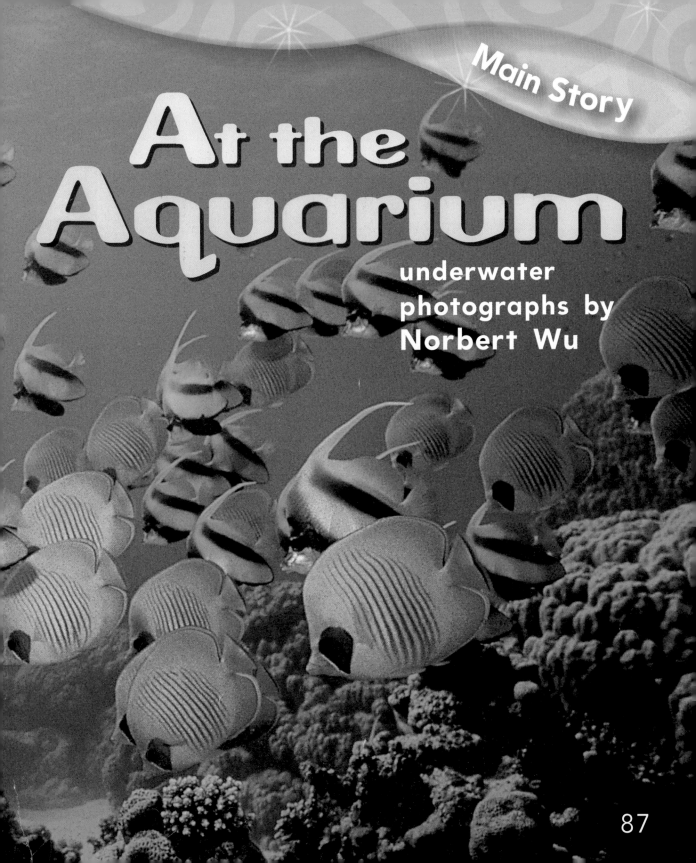

At the Aquarium

underwater
photographs by
Norbert Wu

We are on a class trip.

We will see lots and lots of fish.

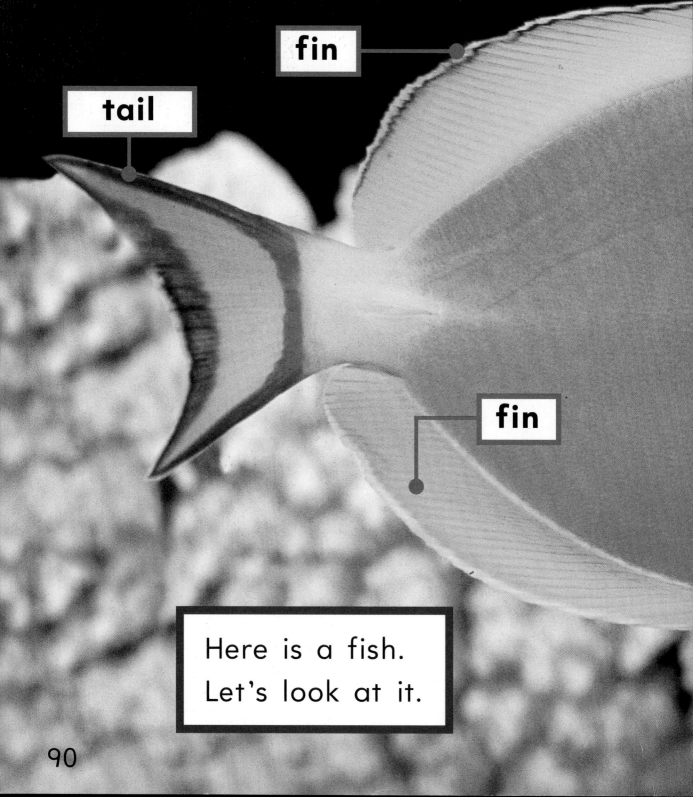

fin

tail

fin

Here is a fish.
Let's look at it.

90

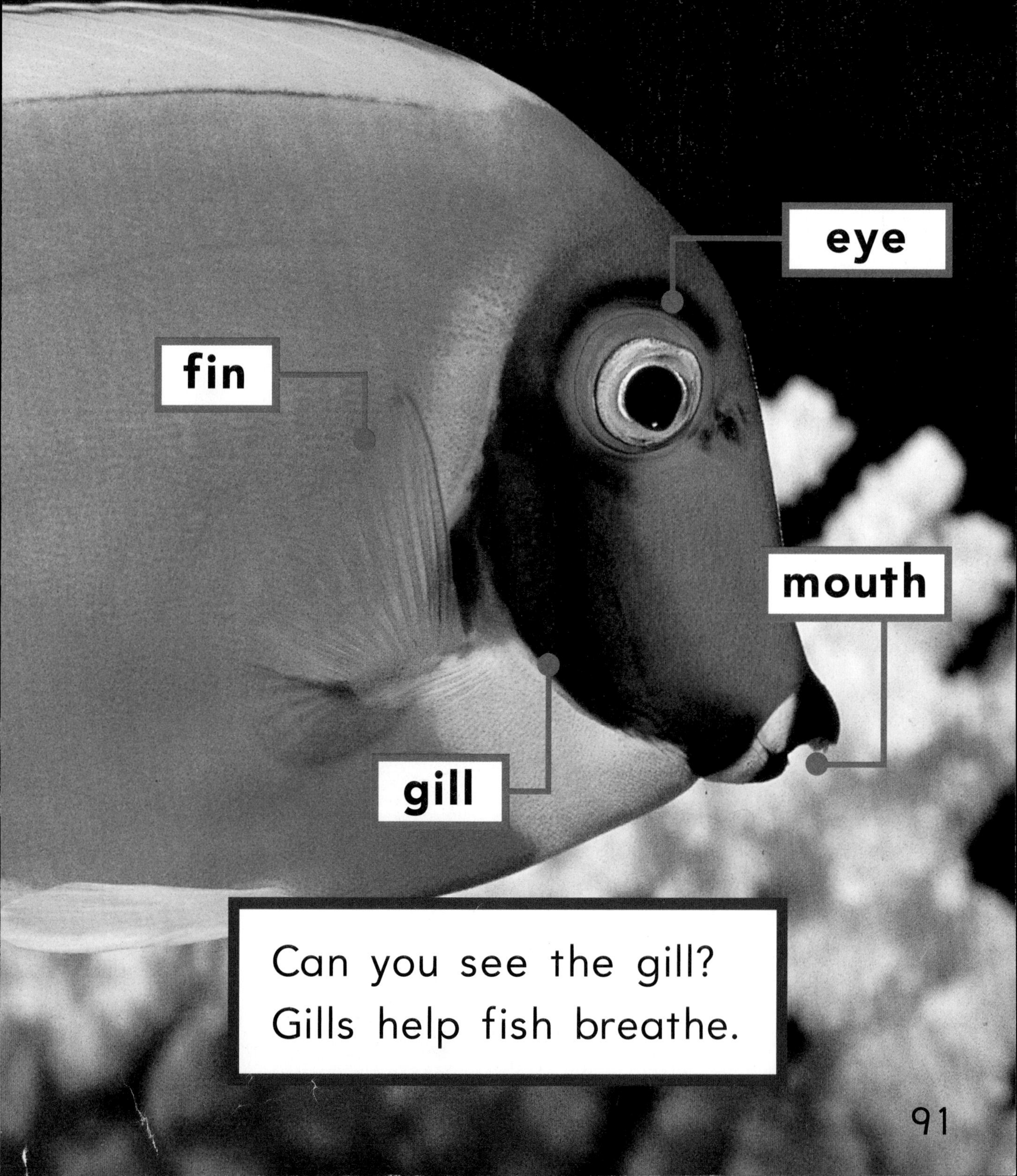

eye

fin

mouth

gill

Can you see the gill?
Gills help fish breathe.

Let's look at fins and tails.
Fins and tails help fish swim well.

Some fins look like fans.

Fish can have lots of colors.
Look! One is green and blue.
One has a black dot on its fin.

We like looking at all the colors.

What do fish eat?
Many eat plants.
Some eat fish.

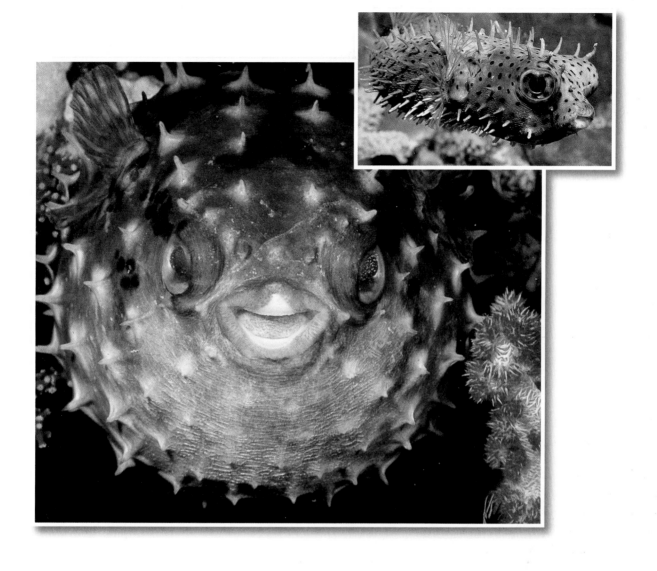

Here's a funny fish.
It has a trick.
It can puff up to get a big fish
to go away.

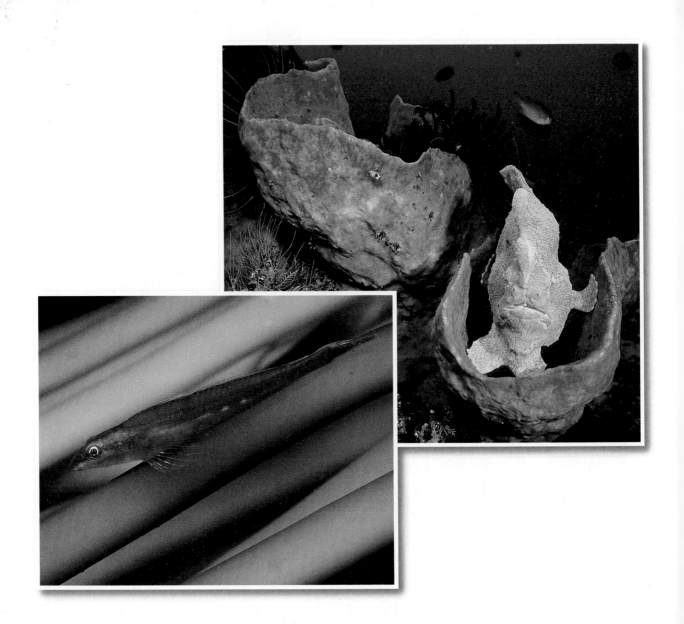

We see two fish. Can you?
One looks like a rock.
One is in the sea grass.

A sea horse can grab on
to a sea plant.

Crabs and sea slugs live
on sand and rocks.
A crab has legs.
It can run fast.

A brown otter also lives here.
It can swim on its back.

We stop next to a big tank
and see dolphins swim.
It's fun to go on a trip here!

fairy basslet

parrotfish

porcupine fish

clownfish

lionfish

sea horse

What did you like best?

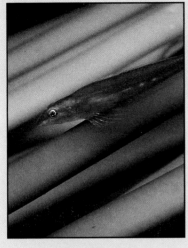  

clingfish **crab** **sea otter**

frogfish **sea slug** **dolphins**

Think About the Story

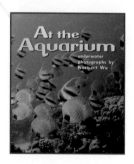

At the Aquarium

1 How are the fish in the story different from each other?

2 Tell two things you learned about fish in this story.

3 Which fish would you like to learn more about? Why?

Retell the Story

Pretend you are a guide at the aquarium. Tell classmates what they will see there.

Writing

Write a Description

Which fish or animal in the story is your favorite? Write a sentence about it.

I like the porcupine fish because it is funny.

Read Together

WHY SUN AND MOON LIVE IN THE SKY

based on an African Tale

Characters

Narrator   Sun   Moon   Sea

Many years ago, Sun and Moon lived in a house. Sea never came to visit. The house was too small.

 So Sun and Moon built a BIG house. Sea and all his sea animals took a trip there.

 We are here to visit.

 Hello, Sea. Come in!

 Sea rushed in with fish and other sea animals. Soon Sun and Moon felt water up to their ears.

Can I bring in some more of my sea animals?

Yes!

Let's all go in!

Water came up to the roof.
Sun and Moon had to go up into
the blue sky, and that's where
they still live today.

Family and Friends

Little pictures
Hang above me.
Pictures of the folks
Who love me.
Mom and Dad
And Uncle Jack,
They love me...
I love them back.

by Arnold Lobel

Stories to Read

1 Get Set Story **2** Main Story **3** Social Studies Link

Realistic
Fiction

Realistic
Fiction

Nonfiction

Words to Know

children	mother	black
come	people	block
family	picture	Fluff
father	your	plan
loves		

Fluff Is Missing!

by Jui Ishida

My cat Fluff ran away. I called
him, but Fluff did not come back.

Max and I had a plan to find Fluff.
We had to get lots of people to
help look for him.

Missing: Family Cat

Fluff is a brown and black cat.

He has a red tag on his neck.

He loves children and dogs.

Fluff will sit on your lap.

Call 555-5555 if you see Fluff.

FLUFF

We added a picture of Fluff.

Max and I left lots and lots
of papers on the block.

"Your plan did it!" said my father.
"We got a call," said my mother.
"Fluff is back!"

Meet the Author

Pat Cummings likes to write family stories. She has a brother and two sisters who have always been her best friends.

Meet the Illustrator

Fred Willingham has always loved to draw people. When he was little, he drew comic book characters.

122

Go Away, Otto!

written by **Pat Cummings**

illustrated by
Fred Willingham

"Is Gran here yet, Dad?" asked Fred.
"Not yet," said Dad.

"Your mother is picking up Gran,"
Dad said.

"Let's clean up for Gran's visit,"
said Dad. "Here is a plan."

"Fix up your beds. Also, pick some pictures Gran will like."

"My bed is first," said Fred. "I will fluff the pillows."
"Can I help?" asked Otto.

"What a mess!" yelled Fred.
"Go away, Otto!"

"I will find pictures of people in the family," said Fred.
"Can I help?" asked Otto.

"What a mess!" yelled Fred.
"Go away, Otto!"

"Dad," Fred said, "Otto is not helping."

"Otto is not a big kid like you,"
said Dad. "He is doing his best."

"Where is Otto?" asked Dad.
"I will find him," said Fred.

"I see lots of blocks, black trucks,
and animals," said Fred.

"I am sorry I yelled at you,"
said Fred. "What a mess!
Can I help?"
"OK," Otto said. "You can
help me play!"

"Gran is here!" said Dad.

"Here are the children I love,"
said Gran. "Come get a big hug."

"Come here, Gran," said Fred.

"Here's a funny picture of Otto
and me at camp," Fred said.
"You kids look just like your
father," said Gran.

"You and Otto have lots of fun,"
said Gran.
"Yes, we do," said Fred. "We are
best pals."

Think About the Story

**Go Away,
Otto!**

1 How are Fred and Otto the same? How are they different?

2 Why did Fred tell Otto that he was sorry?

3 What would you do if you had a brother who acted like Otto?

Retell the Story

Tell what happened in the beginning, the middle, and the end of the story.

Writing

Write a Sentence

Write a sentence that tells something Fred and Otto can do together.

Fred and Otto can play a game.

Helping at Home

All the people in a family
can help around the house.
Children your age can help,
too. How can you help?

There are lots of things you can do. You can make your bed. You can pick up your toys and clothes every day.

Maybe you can help with the cooking. You can set the table and clean up, too. You can even help dry the dishes.

If you have pets, you can help take care of them. Everyone in a family can work together. How do you help your family at home?

Stories to Read

1 Get Set Story

Realistic
Fiction

2 Main Story

Realistic
Fiction

3 Social Studies Link

Nonfiction

Words to Know

friends	she	knelt
girl	sing	rest
know	today	sign
play	write	snack
read	best	

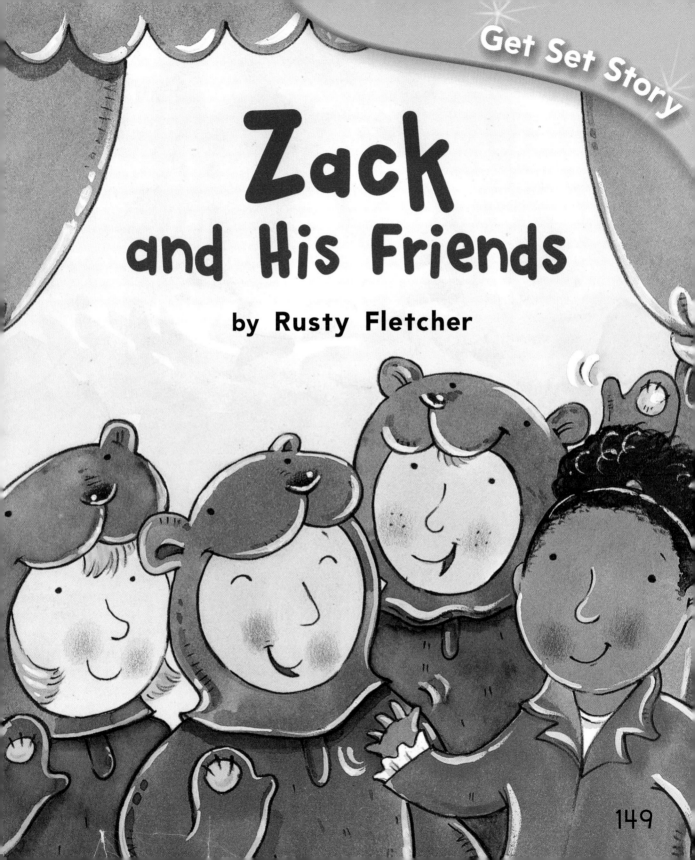

Zack
and His Friends

by Rusty Fletcher

Zack's best friends are Glenn, Ann, and Pat. They play a lot.

Zack and his friends acted in a
class play today. Zack got to
write a sign. Read and see if
you know what play they did.

Pat, Glenn, and Zack acted as
three animals. Ann acted as a
girl. She got to sing.

The girl went in and had a snack.
She said, "One cup is hot, one cup
is cold, and one cup is OK."

The girl had a rest. The animals
got back.
An animal knelt at the bed and
yelled, "Look who is in my bed!"

The girl jumped up and ran.

What play did the kids do?

Eve Bunting

Tracy Sabin

Meet the Author

Eve Bunting has three children and five grandchilden. She gets her story ideas from things that happen in real life.

Meet the Illustrator

Tracy Sabin has four children. He says, "I like to draw what the characters in the story are feeling."

Two Best Friends

written by **Eve Bunting**

illustrated by **Tracy Sabin**

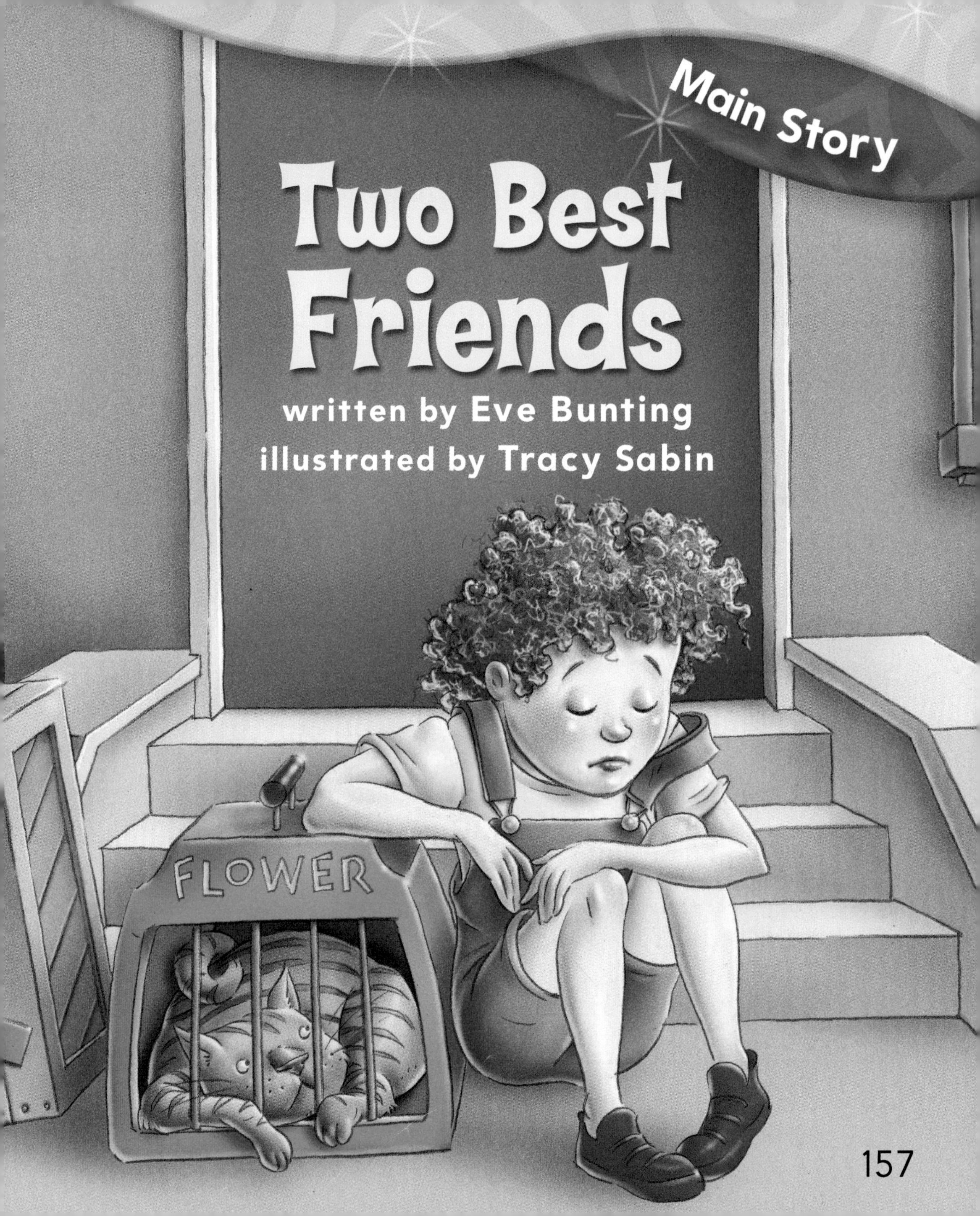

FLOWER

Chapter 1

Peg's dad packed the last big box.

"I will miss you," Peg said.
"I will miss you, too," said Jan.

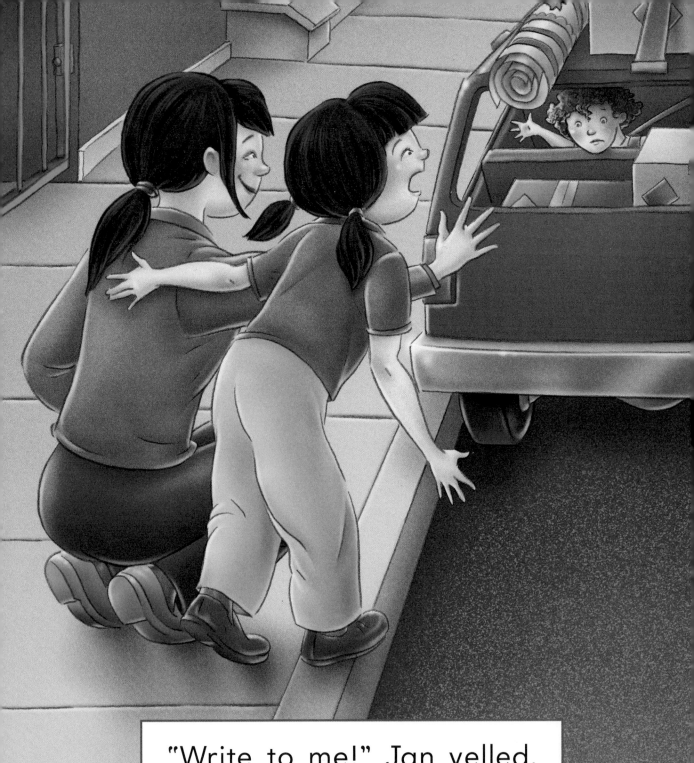

"Write to me!" Jan yelled.

"I know you will find new friends,"
Mom said.
"A new friend is not Jan," Peg said.

"Let's stop for a rest and a snack," said Mom.

"Smile for a picture," said Dad.
Peg smiled, but she still felt sad.

Chapter 2

14
FROST
STREET
APARTMENTS

"Here is the sign," said Mom.
"We are here!"

A black cat ran up to Flower.
Peg's mom knelt to pet the cat.
"Flower has a friend," Mom said.

"Bud! Bud!" Kim called.

"Hi," Kim said. "I am looking for my cat, Bud."

"Hi," Peg said. "Bud is in here. He just met my cat, Flower. You have a Bud, and I have a Flower!"

"Let's play," said Kim.

Peg and Kim have lots of fun.

The girls sing.

They hop and jump.

Peg and Kim dress up.

The girls read some books.

"I will write to Jan," Peg said.

Dear Jan,

Flower and I met new friends today.
Flower met Bud, and I met Kim.
We like it here, but we miss you a lot.

Love,

Peg

"Did you have fun today?"
Mom asked.

"Yes," said Peg. "I am glad
I have two best friends."

Think About the Story

Two Best Friends

1 Is Peg's new home in the city or the country? How do you know?

2 How did Peg feel at the beginning and at the end of the story?

3 What advice would you give Peg about making new friends?

Retell the Story

Tell what happened in the story. Use props, such as toy cats and books.

Write a Card

Make a card for Peg, Jan, or Kim. Write a sentence in the card.

Dear Peg,

How Mail Gets to You

Do you know how a letter gets
from place to place? People write
letters and put them in mailboxes.
Mail carriers bring the letters to
post offices.

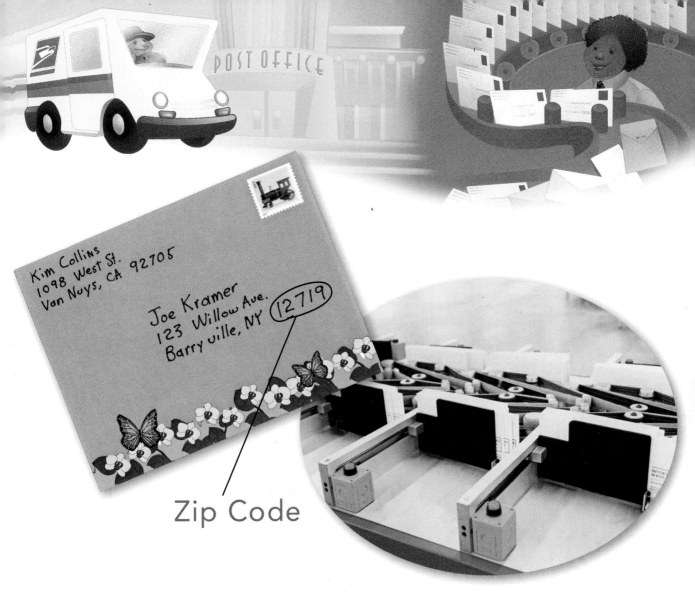

Zip Code

The zip code tells a machine which city or town a letter is going to. The machine puts together letters that have the same zip code.

179

Mail trucks pick up the mail at the post office. Some trucks bring mail to planes. That mail goes far away. Other trucks bring mail to post offices close by.

Mail carriers deliver the mail to the address on the envelope. That's how a letter gets to you!

Stories to Read

1 Get Set Story

2 Main Story

3 Social Studies Link

Fantasy

Realistic
Fiction

Nonfiction

Words to Know

car	hurt	would
down	learn	just
hear	their	must
hold	walk	scrub

Dad's Big Plan

by John Steven Gurney

"Here we are, kids!" Dad yelled.
"Just walk. Do not run. The sand
is hot, but it will not hurt."

"Would you like to hear my big
plan?" asked Dad.
"Yes," yelled Mick and Stef.
Two gulls learn Dad's plan, too.

"We must dig," said Dad.
Mick and Stef dug and dug.
"I will pat down the sand,"
Dad added.

Mick and Stef picked up rocks.
"I can hold lots and lots of rocks,"
Stef said.

Mick jumped up to drip wet sand
on top. The gulls helped, too.
Dad got their picture.

Mick and Stef had to scrub away
the sand at the car.
"Did you have fun?" Dad asked.
"Yes!" they yelled.

Meet the Author
Joseph Bruchac is a storyteller who has written many children's books. He loves dogs and is always learning from them.

Meet the Illustrator
G. Brian Karas knows that dogs can get into all kinds of trouble. He has his own big dog named Otto.

190

Dog School

written by
Joseph Bruchac

illustrated by
G. Brian Karas

Spritz is my dog. She likes to
hear me read.

Spritz likes a scrub in the tub, and she loves to go for a walk.

Spritz is a pest, too. She does
not sit and stay. Plus, she likes
to chase Miss Duff's car down
the street.

One day, Spritz dug up my mom's
flower bed. "Stop, Spritz!" I yelled.
"You are a bad dog." Spritz
looked hurt and sad.

Mom said, "Spritz is not a bad dog.
She just has to learn. Let's go to
a school for dogs."

Six people and their dogs went to
the dog school, too. Some people
looked like their dogs!

Spritz did not do well in class.

Every dog learned to sit and stay,
but not Spritz. Would Spritz learn
to sit and stay?

Would Spritz learn to sit and stay?

Today is the last class. The dogs
must sit and stay to pass the test.

I had to hold Spritz's leash.
"Sit," I said. Spritz sat.

"Stay," I said. I walked away.
Spritz stayed still.

Spritz DID learn!
She passed the test!

"You did it!" said Mom.

Spritz jumped up and knocked
me down. She licked my face.
"You are not just a pet," I said.
"You are my best friend!"

Think About the Story

Dog School

 1. Why did Spritz have to go to dog school?

 2. How was Spritz different in the first class and the last class?

3. Would you like to have Spritz for a pet? Why?

Retell the Story

Act out the story with a partner. Start at the beginning. Take turns being the boy and Spritz.

Make a Poster

Draw a poster that shows something you would like to teach Spritz to do. Write a sentence on your poster.

I will teach Spritz to get the paper.

DOG WALKS • UNIQUE GIFTS • DOGGIE BED & BREAKFAST

Daycare for Dogs

Have you ever heard of daycare for dogs? Many people bring their dogs to daycare. Some dogs even take a bus to get there.

Dogs keep busy at doggie daycare. They may splash with other dogs in a pool. They may also take walks. When a dog gets tired, it can stretch out for a nap.

At doggie daycare, dogs have lots
of room to play. Dogs can go
outside to run and jump. They can
play inside, too. Dogs can even
get groomed at daycare.

Dogs have lots of fun at doggie daycare, but they are happy to see their families at the end of the day.

Animals in the Cold

DECODABLE WORDS

Target Skills:

double final consonants
will

final consonants (*s* as /z/, *ck*)
buds, is, pick

plurals with *s*
buds, lots, pups

blending more short *a* words
and, can

Words Using Kindergarten Review Skills
a, big, cub, den, dig, dip, fox, get, hot, in, it, its, not, sun, up, wet

HIGH-FREQUENCY WORDS

New
animal, animals, birds, cold, fall, flowers, full, look, of, see

Previously Taught
are, do, here, for, go, live, the, they

Seasons

DECODABLE WORDS

Target Skills:

double final consonants
buzz, eggs, grass, pass, will

final consonants (*s* as /z/, *ck*)
buck, buds, ducks, eggs, has, is, kick, pick, quack

plurals with *s*
buds, ducks, eggs, lots, nests, nuts, pups

blending more short *a* words
and, at, can, fat, grass, has, nap, pass, quack

Words Using Previously Taught Skills
a, big, den, end, fox, get, hop, hot, in, it, jump, mud, not, pond, red, run, set, sip, sun, up, wet

HIGH-FREQUENCY WORDS

New
animal, animals, birds, cold, flower, flowers, fall, full, look, of, see

Kindergarten Review
play

Previously Taught
are, do, for, go, here, the, they, three, to, too, two, where, who

STORY VOCABULARY

bear, insects, leaves, rain, south, spring, summer, trees, winter

Ham and Eggs

Target Skills:

verb endings -s, -ed, -ing
fixed, licked, yelled

possessives ('s)
Jack's

blending more short i words
bit, fixed, his, is, it, licked, lips, will

Words Using Previously Taught Skills
a, and, at, can, Dad, eggs, fun, had, ham,
Jack, let, not, pen, Ted, up, us, yum

HIGH-FREQUENCY WORDS

New
all, called, eat, eating, every, first, never,
paper, shall, why

Previously Taught
go, have, here, I, of, said, to, we, what, you

Miss Jill's Ice Cream Shop

DECODABLE WORDS

Target Skills:

verb endings -s, -ed, -ing
added, asked, bumped, dumped, filled,
fixed, licked, yelled

possessives ('s)
Bill's, Jack's, Jill's

blending more short i words
big, Bill, Bill's, filled, fixed, his, in, is, it, Jill,
Jill's, lick, licked, lips, mint, Miss, will

Words Using Previously Taught Skills
a, and, at, can, fell, get, had, help, Jack,
lots, mess, not, nuts, on, plum, ran, run,
top, up, went, yes, yum

HIGH-FREQUENCY WORDS

New
all, call, eat, eating, every, first, never, paper,
shall, why

Kindergarten Review
she

Previously Taught
animals, do, falling, for, go, have, he, here, I,
likes, look, of, said, the, to, too, what, you

STORY VOCABULARY

cone, dish, green, kind, ice cream,
napkins, shop, try, wish

The Trip

Target Skills:

consonant clusters with *r*
grab, grass, trip

contractions with -*'s*
it's, let's

Words Using Previously Taught Skills
a, added, and, at, big, bus, cab, cat, cats, Dad, get, hop, in, is, Mom, on, pass, Puff, sat, Tip, went, yelled

New
also, blue, brown, colors, funny, green, like, many, some

Previously Taught
all, are, go, here, I, look, said, see, the, we, what, where

At the Aquarium

Target Skills:

consonant clusters with *r*
crab, crabs, grab, grass, trick, trip

contractions with -*'s*
it's, let's

Words Using Previously Taught Skills
a, and, at, back, best, big, black, can, class, did, dot, fans, fast, fins, fun, get, gills, has, help, in, is, it, legs, lots, next, on, plant, plants, puff, rock, run, sand, slug, stop, swim, tank, up, well, will

New
also, blue, brown, colors, funny, green, like, many, some

Previously Taught
all, are, away, do, eat, go, have, here, here's, live, look, looking, looks, of, one, see, the, to, two, we, what, you

breathe, dolphins, fish, otter, sea, sea horse, tails

218

Fluff Is Missing!

Target Skills:

consonant clusters with l
black, block, Fluff, plan

blending more short o words
block, dogs, got, lots, not, on

Words Using Previously Taught Skills
a, added, and, back, but, cat, did, dogs, get, had, has, help, him, his, if, is, it, lap, left, Max, missing, neck, ran, red, sit, tag, will

HIGH-FREQUENCY WORDS

New
children, come, family, father, loves, mother, people, picture, your

Previously Taught
away, brown, call, called, find, for, he, I, look, my, of, papers, said, see, the, to, we, you

Go Away, Otto!

DECODABLE WORDS

Target Skills:

consonant clusters with l
black, blocks, fluff, plan

blending more short o words
blocks, lots, not

Words Using Previously Taught Skills
a, am, and, asked, at, bed, beds, best, big, camp, can, Dad, fix, Fred, fun, get, Gran, Gran's, help, helping, him, his, hug, in, is, just, kid, let's, mess, OK, pals, pick, picking, trucks, up, will, yelled, yes, yet

HIGH-FREQUENCY WORDS

New
children, come, family, father, love, mother, people, pictures, your

Kindergarten Review
play

Previously Taught
also, animals, are, away, do, doing, find, first, for, funny, go, have, he, here, here's, I, like, look, me, my, of, said, see, some, the, we, what, where, you

STORY VOCABULARY

clean, pillows, sorry, visit

Zack and His Friends

DECODABLE WORDS

Target Skills:

consonant clusters with s
best, rest, snack

silent consonants kn, wr, gn
knelt, sign

blending more short e words
bed, best, Glenn, knelt, rest, went, yelled

Words Using Previously Taught Skills
a, acted, an, and, Ann, as, at, back, class, cup, did, got, had, his, hot, if, in, is, jumped, kids, lot, OK, Pat, ran, up, Zack, Zack's

HIGH-FREQUENCY WORDS

New
friends, girl, know, play, read, she, sing, today, write

Previously Taught
animal, animals, are, cold, do, look, my, one, said, see, the, they, three, to, what, who, you

Two Best Friends

DECODABLE WORDS

Target Skills:

consonant clusters with s
asked, best, just, last, rest, snack, still, stop

silent consonants kn, wr, gn
knelt, sign

blending more short e words
best, dress, felt, knelt, let's, met, Peg, Peg's, pet, rest, yelled, yes

Words Using Previously Taught Skills
a, am, and, big, black, box, Bud, but, cat, Dad, did, fun, glad, has, hop, in, is, it, Jan, Kim, lot, lots, miss, Mom, not, packed, ran, sad, up, will

HIGH-FREQUENCY WORDS

New
friend, friends, girls, know, play, read, she, sing, today, write

Previously Taught
are, called, find, Flower, for, have, he, here, I, jump, like, looking, love, me, my, of, picture, said, some, the, they, to, too, two, we, you

STORY VOCABULARY

books, dear, new, sign, smile, smiled

Dad's Big Plan

Target Skills:

triple clusters
scrub

blending more short *u* words
but, dug, fun, gulls, jumped, just, must,
run, scrub, up

Words Using Previously Taught Skills
added, and, asked, at, big, can, Dad,
Dad's, did, dig, drip, got, had, helped, hot,
is, it, kids, lots, Mick, not, on, pat, pick,
plan, rocks, sand, Stef, top, wet, will,
yelled, yes

New
car, down, hear, hold, hurt, learn, their, walk,
would

Previously Taught
are, away, do, have, here, I, like, my, of,
picture, said, the, they, to, too, two, we, you

Dog School

Target Skills:

triple clusters
scrub, Spritz, Spritz's

blending more short *u* words
but, Duff's, dug, jumped, just, must, plus,
scrub, tub, up

Words Using Previously Taught Skills
a, and, bad, bed, best, class, did, dog, dogs,
had, has, in, is, it, knocked, last, let's,
licked, Miss, Mom, mom's, not, pass,
passed, pest, pet, sad, sat, sit, six, still, stop,
test, well, went, yelled, yip

New
car, down, hear, hold, hurt, learn, learned,
their, walk, walked, would

Previously Taught
are, away, do, does, every, flower, for, friend,
go, I, like, likes, looked, loves, me, my, one,
people, read, said, she, some, the, to, today,
too, you

chase, day, face, leash, school, stay,
stayed, street

a	find	like	sing
all	first	live	some
also	five	look	the
and	flower	love	their
animal	for	many	they
are	four	me	three
away	friend	mother	to
bird	full	my	today
blue	funny	never	too
brown	girl	not	two
call	go	of	upon
car	green	on	walk
children	have	once	we
cold	he	one	what
color	hear	paper	where
come	here	people	who
do	hold	picture	why
does	hurt	play	would
down	I	pull	write
eat	in	read	you
every	is	said	your
fall	jump	see	
family	know	shall	
father	learn	she	

Decoding skills taught to date: consonants *m, s, t, c;* short *a;* consonants *n, f, p; b, r, h, g;* short *i;* consonants *d, w, l, x;* short *o;* consonants *k, v, y;* short *e;* consonants *q, j, z;* short *u;* double final consonants; final consonants (*s* as /z/, *ck*); plurals with *-s;* blending more short *a* words; verb endings *-s, -ed, -ing;* possesives (*'s*); blending more short *i* words; consonant clusters with *r;* contractions with *-'s;* consonant clusters with *l;* blending more short *o* words; consonant clusters with *s;* blending more short *e* words; silent consonants *kn, wr, gn;* triple clusters; blending more short *u* words

Acknowledgments

Go Away, Otto!, by Pat Cummings. Copyright © by Pat Cummings. Published by arrangement with the author.

"Little Pictures" from *Whiskers & Rhymes*, by Arnold Lobel. Copyright © 1985 by Arnold Lobel. Reprinted by permission of HarperCollins Publishers.

"Sleeping Outdoors" from *Rhymes About Us*, by Marchette Chute, published in1974 by E.P. Dutton. Copyright © 1974 by Marchette Chute. Reprinted by permission of Elizabeth Hauser.

Credits

Photography

3, 5 © HMCo/Film Archive. 7, 8 © HMCo/Tony Scarpetta. 10–11 David Bradley Photography/ Chris Butler. Illustration. 11 (m) © HMCo/Film Archive. 12 (bl, mr) Joseph Van Os/The Image Bank/Getty Images. 13 Kevin Schafer/The Image Bank/Getty Images. 14 Norbert Rosing/National Geographic/Getty Images. 15 (tl) Paul Nicklen/ National Geographic/Getty Images. (tr) David E. Myers/Stone/Getty Images. (bl) Carleton Ray/ Photo Researchers. (br) Eastcott Momatiuk/The Image Bank/Getty Images. (bkgd) Julie Habel/ Corbis. 16 (tl) Dan Guravich/Photo Researchers. (br-bkgd) Norbert Rosing/National Geographic/ Getty Images. (br-inset) Wayne R. Bilenduke/The Image Bank/Getty Images. (bkgd) Julie Habel/ Corbis. 17 (tl) Art Wolfe, Inc. (bkgd) Solvin Zankl/ Stone/Getty Images. 18–19 Johnny Johnson/ Animals Animals. 40 (bmr), (br) Rich Iwasaki/ Getty Images. (bl) Claire Rydell/Index Stock. (bml) Richard Shiell/Animals Animals. 42 © HMCo/G. K. & Vikki Hart/Photodisc. 43 RubberBall Productions. 44 Chase Swift/Corbis. 45 David Zelick/The Image Bank/Getty Images. 72 (bl) Burke/Triolo/Brand X Pictures/PictureQuest. (br) C. Squared Studios/ Photodisc/Getty Images. 74–75 © Nial Yager Washington State University Creamery. 76 (tl) Richard T. Nowitz/National Geographic. (tr) Juan Silva/The Image Bank/Getty Images. 77 (tr) © Nial Yager Washington State University Creamery. (br) Richard Gross/Corbis. (bl) Michael Newman/PhotoEdit. 86–87 Norbert Wu/www.norbertwu.com. 88–89 (bkgd) George Grall/© National Aquarium in Baltimore Aquarium. (inset) © HMCo/Ken Karp. 90–101 Norbert Wu/www.norbertwu.com. 102 (inset) © HMCo/ Ken Karp. 103 (inset) Docwhite/Taxi/Getty Images. 104 Norbert Wu/www.norbertwu.com. 105 (tl, tm, tr, bl, bm) Norbert Wu/www.norbertwu.com. (br-bkgd) Tom Benoit/ Superstock. (br-inset) Docwhite/Taxi/Getty Images. 106 Norbert Wu/www.norbertwu.com. 112–113 © Stephen Simpson/Taxi/Getty Images. 113 (m) © HMCo/Tony Scarpetta. 142 Masterfile. 144 (l) Ronnie Kaufman/Corbis. (m) Roy Morsch/ Corbis. (r) Chip Henderson/ Index Stock. 145 (l) Michael Newman/PhotoEdit. (m) Myrleen Ferguson Cate/PhotoEdit. (r) Laura Dwight/ PhotoEdit. 146 Ariel Skelley/Corbis. 147 Kris Coppieters/Superstock. 176 DigitalVision /PictureQuest. 178 (l) Tony Freeman/PhotoEdit. (r-inset) Sonda Dawes/The Image Works. (r-bkgd) Lawrence Migdale/Photo Researchers. 179 (r) Courtesy of the U S Census Bureau. 180 (r) Lawrence Manning/Corbis. 181 (l) Henry Diltz/ Corbis. (r) International Stock/ImageState. 210 Comstock Images. 212 Cami Johnson Photography. 213 (l) B. Toby/ Stock Connection/ PictureQuest. (m) Creatas/ PictureQuest. (r) Gail Shumway/Bruce Coleman. 214 (tl) Kevin R. Morris/Corbis. (m) Frederick Ayer III/Photo Researchers. (br) Ian & Gail M. Shumway/Bruce Coleman. 215 David Schmidt/ Masterfile.

Illustration

12–19 (borders) Patrick Gnan. 20–40 Ashley Wolff. 42–45 Jimmy Pickering. 46–53 Kathryn